Bend and Stretch

LEARNING ABOUT YOUR BONES AND MUSCLES

WRITTEN BY PAMELA HILL NETTLETON
ILLUSTRATED BY BECKY SHIPE

Thanks to our advisers for their expertise, research, and advice:
Angela Busch, M.D., All About Children Pediatrics, Minneapolis, Minnesota

Susan Kesselring, M.A., Literacy Educator
Rosemount-Apple Valley-Eagan (Minnesota) School District

PICTURE WINDOW BOOKS
MINNEAPOLIS, MINNESOTA

Managing Editor: Bob Temple
Creative Director: Terri Foley
Editor: Kristin Thoennes Keller
Editorial Adviser: Andrea Cascardi
Copy Editor: Laurie Kahn
Designer: Melissa Voda
Page production: The Design Lab
The illustrations in this book were rendered digitally.

Picture Window Books
151 Good Counsel Drive
P.O. Box 669
Mankato, MN 56002-0669
1-877-845-8392
www.picturewindowbooks.com

Printed in the United States of America.

Library of Congress Cataloging-in-Publication Data
Nettleton, Pamela Hill.
   Bend and stretch: learning about your bones and muscles / by Pamela Hill
Nettleton ; illustrated by Becky Shipe.
      p. cm. — (The amazing body)
Summary: An introduction to the different muscles and bones in the human
body and how they function. Includes bibliographical references and index.
   ISBN 978-1-4048-0256-8 (hardcover)
   ISBN 978-1-4048-0507-1 (paperback)
1. Musculoskeletal system—Juvenile literature. [1. Muscular system.
2. Skeleton.] I. Shipe, Becky, 1977– ill. II. Title.
   QP301 .N44 2004
   612.7—dc22   2003018186

Tap your foot. Wave your hand at a friend. How does your body do that? It uses bones and muscles!

Inside of your body, you have a skeleton made of bones. Bones are strong and hard. Bones help hold your body upright.

Muscles are like bundles of stretchy rubber bands that hold your bones together. They are attached to your bones and help them move.

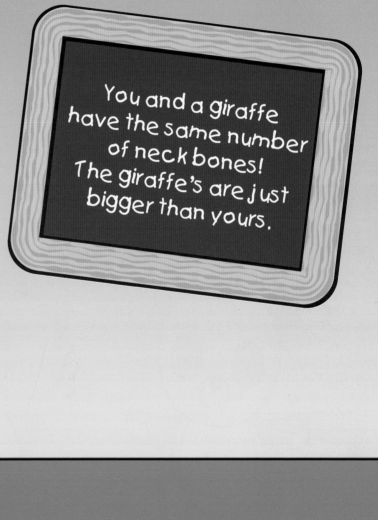

You and a giraffe have the same number of neck bones! The giraffe's are just bigger than yours.

When you were a baby, you had more bones than you do now. Babies have about 300 bones that are soft and flexible, like firm rubber.

Some bones join together as you get older. Your bones also get harder as you grow. Adults have 206 bones that are hard and strong.

Around age 25, all of your bones will be hard. Then you stop growing.

If your skeleton were made of metal, you would be too heavy to move! Your bones are strong but light.

Bones are light and easy to move because they are not solid inside. Instead, they are filled with a jelly-like substance called bone marrow. Bone marrow's job is to make new blood cells.

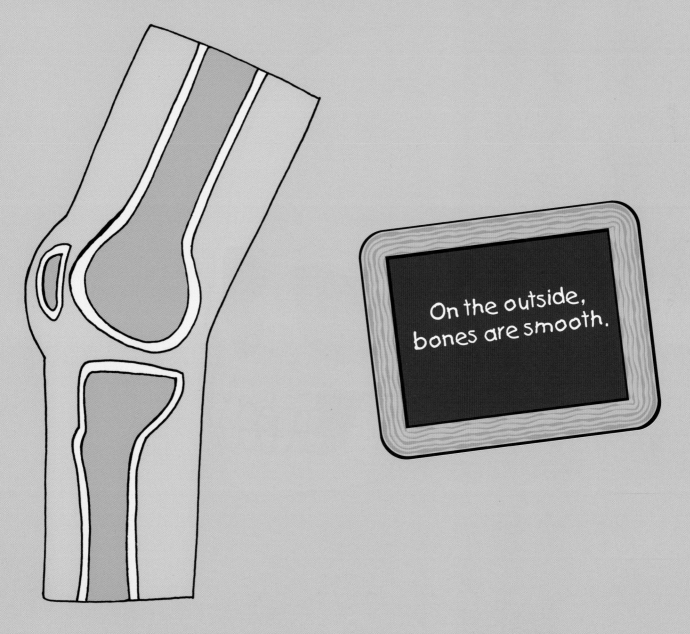

On the outside, bones are smooth.

Bones protect the important soft parts
of your body. Your skull protects your brain.

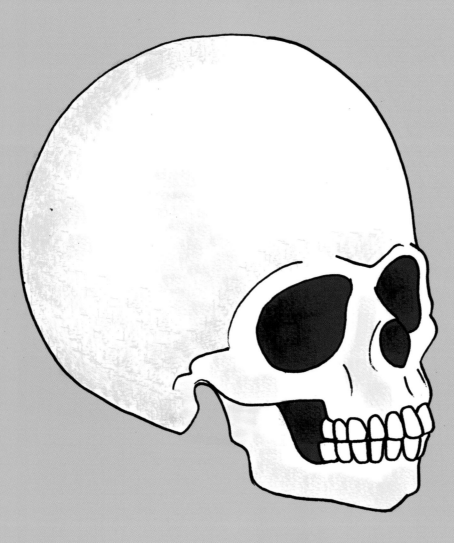

Your rib cage protects your heart, lungs, and stomach.

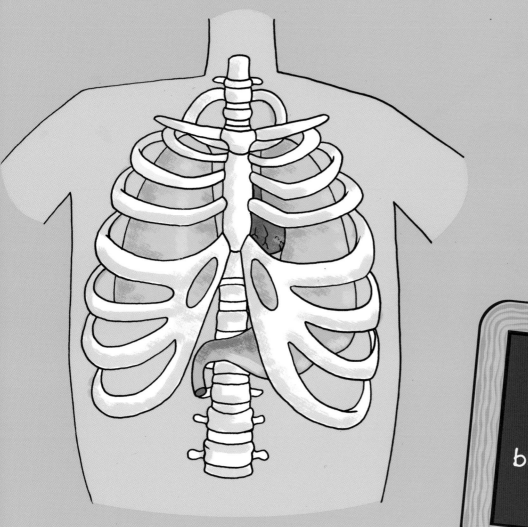

Your longest bone is your thigh bone. Your smallest is behind your eardrum.

Grab your elbow. Feel it bend and move.
Your elbow is a joint. A joint is a place where
two bones meet.

A joint is a good place to see how muscles work. Muscles attach to bones on each side of a joint. The muscles stretch and shrink as the joint is straightened and bent.

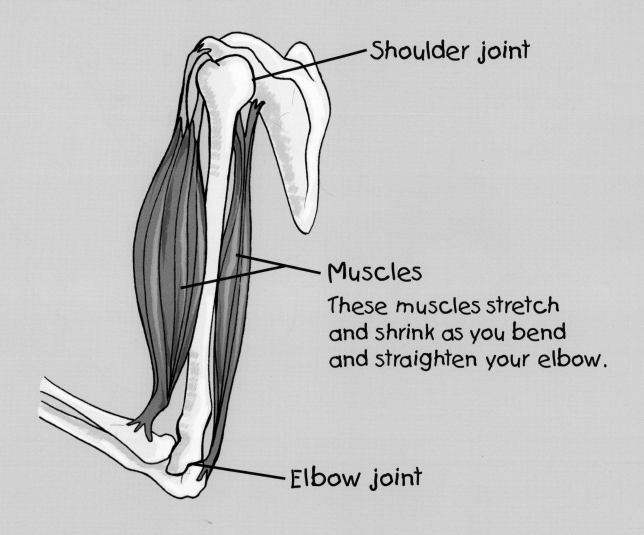

Shoulder joint

Muscles

These muscles stretch and shrink as you bend and straighten your elbow.

Elbow joint

Muscles that help your skeleton move are called skeletal muscles. These muscles get bigger and stronger when you make them work hard.

That's why figure skaters have big leg muscles.
That's why basketball players have big arm muscles.

Did you ever break a bone? Then you know that your bones are alive and growing. They can mend and get better.

Did you ever pull a muscle? Pulling a muscle is actually tearing your muscle. Muscles can heal like bones.

Some muscles work on their own. Your heart is one muscle that does this.

Exercise is good for your muscles. Ride a bike. Chase a ball. Moving keeps your muscles strong.

Exercise is good for bones, too. Bones and muscles also like it when you eat right and drink lots of water. That helps them to work well.

Make a face! Your face has more than 30 muscles.

Take good care of your bones. Wear a helmet when you ride a bike. Wear elbow and knee pads when you skate on skateboards.

What muscles work the hardest? Surprise! Your eye muscles move about 100,000 times each day.

Take good care of your muscles. Stretch them every day. Reach for the sky!

BONES AND MUSCLES

- There are three types of muscles: smooth (like your stomach); cardiac (your heart muscle); and skeletal (the muscles that hold your bones together).

- Your tongue is a group of muscles.

- Tendons are cords that connect bone and muscle.

- Most people have 12 pairs of ribs. Some people have extra ribs.

- Your skull is made up of 30 different bones.

- One foot and ankle has 52 bones. One hand and wrist has 54 bones.

- Your femur is your thigh bone. It is the longest bone in your body.

FIND YOUR JOINTS!

Can you name some joints in your body? Remember, a joint is a place where two bones meet. Most joints are in the places where you can bend. You have more than 230 joints in your body.

Some possible answers: elbows, knees, ankles, wrists, neck, fingers, hips, shoulders, toes

TOOLS OF THE TRADE

To check your bones, your doctor might take an X-ray. An X-ray machine takes pictures through your skin and muscles. Then your doctor looks at the pictures. An X-ray can show a broken or cracked bone.

To check your muscles, your doctor may ask you to twist and bend. She or he will watch to see if it is easy or hard for you.

GLOSSARY

bone (BOHN)—one of the hard white parts that makes up your skeleton

bone marrow (BOHN MA-roh)—the jelly-like material inside of the bone where blood cells are made

joint (JOINT)—the bendable place where two bones meet

muscle (MUHSS-uhl)—a rubbery part of your body that produces movement

skeleton (SKEL-uh-tuhn)—your body's framework of bones

INDEX

babies, 6
bone marrow, 9
brain, 10
exercise, 18–19
heart, 11, 17, 22
joint, 12–13, 23
lungs, 11
rib cage, 11
skeleton, 4, 8, 14
skull, 10, 22
stomach, 11, 22

TO LEARN MORE

At the Library

Barner, Bob. *Dem Bones*. San Francisco: Chronicle Books, 1996.

Seymour, Simon. *Bones: Our Skeletal System.* New York: Morrow Junior Books, 1998.

Seymour, Simon. *Muscles: Our Muscular System.* New York: Morrow Junior Books, 1998.

On the Web

FactHound offers a safe, fun way to find Web sites related to topics in this book. All of the sites on FactHound have been researched by our staff.

1. Visit *www.facthound.com*
2. Type in this special code: 1404802568
3. Click on the FETCH IT button.

Your trusty Fact Hound will fetch the best sites for you!